The
POWER
of

Orchestrated
Knowledge

JOYCE JAY

Pastor of Worship Life Center Church / Mesa, Arizona

KP PUBLISHING COMPANY

The Power of OK: Orchestrated Knowledge

ISBN: 978-1-960001-15-3 (Paperback)
ISBN: 978-1-960001-16-0 (eBook)
Library of Congress Control Number: 2023905654

Editor: Delerice Mackey
Illustrator: Juan Roberts, Creative Lunacy
Literary Director: Sandra Slayton James

Unless otherwise note, Scripture taken from the New King James Version®. Copyright © 1982 by Thomas Nelson. Used by permission. All rights reserved.

Published by:

KP Publishing Company
Publisher of Fiction, Nonfiction & Children's Books
Valencia, CA 91355
www.kp-pub.com
Printed in the United States of America

"To know which way you're going in every dialogue or encounter of life you need two simple letters that demonstrate wisdom."

OK

DEDICATION

I want to dedicate this book to God who has given me a new life through his Son, Jesus Christ, and the guidance of the Holy Spirit.

Wisdom is the principal thing;
Therefore get wisdom.
And in all your getting, get understanding.

PROVERBS 4:7

CONTENTS

INTRODUCTION

When you process your situation and see no way out, just say OK. When you use OK, you rely on the Holy Spirit's guidance to use wisdom and knowledge. This action helps you produce an outcome that cancels arguments and negativity and produces peace and victory.

The O in OK is Orchestrate: to direct your thoughts and plans and give ear to the Holy Spirit. The K in OK is knowledge: once you direct your thoughts, plans, and ear to the Holy Spirit, you receive the wisdom and knowledge of the Holy Spirit on what your next plan of action will be.

In so many situations, I've seen never-ending discussions that have led to frustration, bitterness, resentment, and unforgiveness. When all we had to do was turn this situation in a different direction, to come to a common resolve either right away or later.

Proverbs 4:7 says get wisdom and with all thy getting get an understanding.

The Wisdom = Holy Spirit

Understanding = God

When you say OK, you agree with the enemy in the natural eye, but in the spiritual eye you agree with the Holy Spirit to give you the wisdom, understanding, and redirection in your situation. This gives you the power over the situation thus allowing God to let it work in your favor.

So, I'm saying OK. When you say OK, it does not leave the door open for debate or response. It gives you the opportunity to seek God's face and to watch and pray, and to grab hold of the gifts of the Spirit. It gives you the opportunity to rethink, reevaluate, reposition, redirect, resubmit, and resolve. As you can see, all the words start with re: which is a prefix meaning go back or backward or a backward motion or to retell or recall.

1. **Rethink** = think again
2. **Reevaluate** = evaluate again or differently
3. **Reposition** = place in a different position or alter the position
4. **Redirect** = direct something to a new or different place or purpose

5. **Resubmit** = submit again
6. **Resolve** = settle or find a solution

Isn't this what we want? To ultimately have a resolve or a win-win in every area of our life?

So, in this book this is what we're going to learn:

How to come to a resolve in areas of our lives by the power of two letters, OK.

In my life as a young girl, I was child #6, my "mama's baby" as my older sisters called me. My mom had eight children with my Dad. Growing up, one of my biggest issues was feeling like I was not being heard, No one was listening, and I felt I had a lot to say. I would always have to jump into the conversation loudly with my older siblings because I was the baby, and no one listened to the baby. And then being raised in a family where my parents divorced when I was young, and my mother died when I was 13; and feeling when my Dad and I did encounter, he wouldn't listen either. I felt "Oh! He thinks it's his way or the highway" (speaking from a young teenager's point of view). This caused plenty of arguments and debates, and I felt like I was fighting a losing battle.

I found myself in my adult life interrupting conversations, which turned out to be rude. It left me feeling unimportant, nonexistent, worthless, and not really knowing who I was (which also had a lot to do with losing my mom at the age of 13).

It wasn't until I became an adult and a believer in the Lord Jesus Christ that the Holy Spirit revealed to me my purpose and my worth.

You see, I would go to church feeling alone, and I would ask God why I did not fit in, and one day the Holy Spirit spoke to me and said, "You will never fit in, because I have set you apart for my Glory."

Listening to the Holy Spirit led me to understand the power of OK.

The whole time I was worried about people not listening to me, I never realized that I wasn't listening either (to the Holy Spirit). So finally, the Lord spoke to me and said, "Listen and just say OK and do what I tell you to do."

In the following chapters, I will give you tools and different situations to help you navigate, rethink, and discover ***The Power of OK*** in your everyday life.

OK, Let's Go!

THE POWER OF **OK** IN RELATIONSHIPS

"nevertheless, not my will,
but yours, be done."

LUKE 22:42

Relationships are inevitable. You will have different people you come in contact with; you cannot avoid interacting with others, and why wouldn't you want to interact with others? Even the Father, the Son, and the Holy Spirit work together, and they're One, but have different functions. So likewise, we are all one body of believers with different functions.

We sometimes tend to veer off course and focus on the functions or gifts of others in the kingdom instead of our functions in the body of Christ. We would be further along in our relationship with God and others and in relation to our communication with God if we just said OK to the Holy Spirit and allowed Him to direct our path.

John 16:13-14 states, *"But when he the Spirit of truth has come, he will guide you into all truth, for he will not speak on his own authority, but whatever he hears he will speak, and he will tell you things to come. He will glorify Me, for he will take of what is mine and declare it to you."*

OK = Orchestrated Knowledge, direction. If I knew then what I know now, I would have allowed the Holy Spirit's direction in my thinking. I am reminded of the scripture in I Corinthians 13:11,

When I was a child, I spoke as a child, I understood as a child, I thought as a child: but when I became a man, I put away childish things.

It brings to mind my childhood when my thoughts were all over the place. I think of how I lost my mother at age 13 and could not stand my father. When he would say something, I would be angry and ignore everything he said because he represented hurt, pain, disconnect, and betrayal. I didn't have the power of the Holy Spirit. I didn't know how to say OK to redirect my thinking or to focus on what was good. But, as I began to see later that just saying OK, and the power of it in my life, I wouldn't have hit so many roadblocks in my relationships, even in relating to who I was then. I know who and whose I am today!

It's so funny that sometimes in relationships, I can be, or seem to be, distant or quiet, and it's because I am a studier of people. I really don't do the BFF (Best Friends Forever) thing, and I'll explain that later. Instead, I examine and see how people operate, and then I make my adjustments. I realized early on that you can't change anyone; you can only change how you deal with them. It keeps you safe, and it also keeps them safe.

I remember the relationship that Jesus had with Peter. Jesus knew Peter inside and out. He didn't try to change Peter, but he knew what to expect and made his adjustments. He never stopped using him, but he knew that Peter was predictable and would do something out of pocket - like operating in his emotions. You can't change people; you can only make your adjustments.

———

OK is an excellent response to an unpredictable situation. OK puts you at a stop sign and then helps you seek the Holy Spirit's wisdom to determine the right way and the right approach. So, let's get to the BFF thing since we're talking about relationships and *The Power of OK*.

So, I've had BFFs and have been labeled as someone else's BFF. And it always seemed that I got the short end of the stick. I would give and give and expected the same in return, but I never got it. God finally gave me wisdom after I said, "OK, Lord, help me with this." Well, I was expecting things or had expectations from my BFFs but never discussed those expectations with them to see if they were able to meet them and vice versa. I realized this when I experienced this reaction from someone who called me their BFF. They were expecting things from me that I couldn't fulfill, which was a heavy load to carry. So my BFF is now Jesus and my husband. I know what to expect from them, and they know what to expect from me. I am sure I fall short sometimes, but they love me anyway, and I love them. So you see, I said OK, and God redirected me and gave me wisdom. I love people where they're at. My expectations come from God.

CHAPTER 1: NOTES

THE POWER OF OK IN RELATIONSHIPS

Scripture Readings:

"Father, if it is your will, take this cup away from me; nevertheless, not my will, but yours, be done."

LUKE 22:42

However, when He, the Spirit of truth, has come, He will guide you into all truth; for He will not speak on His own authority, but whatever He hears He will speak; and He will tell you things to come. He will glorify Me, for He will take of what is Mine and declare it to you.

JOHN 16:13-14

When I was a child, I spoke as a child, I understood as a child, I thought as a child, but when I became a man, I put away childish things.

I CORINTHIANS 13:11

Peter answered and said to Him, "Even if all are made to stumble because of You, I will never be made to stumble." Jesus said to him, "Assuredly, I say to you that this night, before the rooster crows, you will deny Me three times."

MATTHEW 26:33-34

1. What relationships have you avoided or not dealt with because of past hurts and pains?

_____

_____

_____

2. Has unforgiveness taken root in your heart towards the people that have hurt you and caused you to avoid other relationships because of your experience? And if yes, has this chapter helped you want to deal with them?

_____

_____

_____

3. Have you had the opportunity to think about why you haven't excelled in life? Is it because of unforgiveness or unresolved issues? And what do you plan to do to operate in forgiveness or to resolve the issue?

_____

_____

_____

4. Are you feeling obligated to fulfill someone else's need in a relationship out of guilt or expectation in a BFF? It is time to break away from unhealthy relationships. What is your plan, if any, to come out of bondage in relationships that are not healthy?

_____

_____

_____

THE POWER OF **OK** IN MARRIAGES

For we do not wrestle against flesh and
blood, but against principalities, against
powers, against the rulers of [a]the darkness
of this age, against spiritual hosts of
wickedness in the heavenly places.

EPHESIANS 6:12

W e all know that marriage is not easy. You have two different people from two different backgrounds. I have been married to my husband, my BFF, for nineteen years, and it was not easy in the beginning. He had his way, and I had mine. I was going to have it my way, and he was not budging with what he wanted. It was my third marriage and his first; I had four children, and he had two.

Pastor Stan says, "There is no way that two believers filled with the Holy Ghost should not be able to come to a resolve." We always did, but it wasn't easy. During our early years, we disagreed a lot. The way I disciplined and the way he disciplined were totally different. We argued about the finances. There was even a time in our marriage when we separated for about a year. During that time of separation, I was able to hear from God. All the disagreements and arguments were a distraction. I was able to listen to God and allow Him to speak to me, and I followed his every direction. He (God) taught me to be quiet and listen.

So, when I was with my four older sisters and older brother, I had to jump into a conversation if I wanted to be heard, and I would get frustrated if I felt no one was listening. So, of course, this spilled over to every relationship or conversation, including my marriage and relationship with my heavenly Father. So, during this time, I learned to say OK and listen to the Holy Spirit. What a revelation! Some of us have that relationship with God now, where we do all the talking without listening.

Before my husband became a Pastor, he went through a pretty rough life of drugs and alcohol addiction, some of which I experienced. It caused a lot of arguing and disagreements, but even in his addiction, God used him. Because of what I went through with him, there were trust issues. I felt even after the addiction, why should I listen to him? Well, God set me straight! He told me one day," That is my son; I called him." I even remember one day when I was complaining about him, and the Lord spoke to me as clearly as day. He said, "Daughter, shut up and do what I told you to do. I got him. That is my son." All I could say was, "OK." That was an OK of agreement and a redirect from the Holy Spirit.

I have learned that God called us to be a wife, husband, or servant, and no matter what my husband was doing, I had to be obedient to what God had called me to do. Now, once he started walking in his deliverance, it did not mean that we agreed right away. But, we learned that when we disagreed, we had to say, "OK, let's table this thing. So, that meant we set it aside and returned to it later. During this time, of course, I'd say OK.

Now, this redirect caused me to consult the Lord, and I would pray, "Lord, you know all things and what's best for us. I know You made my husband head over our house, and You cannot go against creative order. So, whatever You would have us to do, either reveal it to him or give it to me and prepare his heart to receive it."

———

See, after you've said OK, you have to allow the Holy Spirit to give you direction. So, the first thing to do is pray; second, listen; third, follow the instructions and fourth, wait on God's timing. The timing was preparation for God to move in Stan's heart. This way, during the revealing time, you are not angry, you're still being the wife or husband, and the husband is also praying. So, we all agree with what God wants us to do. When you find yourself in a disagreement or conversation where your peace is being disturbed, say OK and lend an ear to the Holy Spirit's direction.

CHAPTER 2: NOTES

THE POWER OF OK IN MARRIAGE

Scripture Readings:

For we do not wrestle against flesh and blood, but against principalities, against powers, against the rulers of [a]the darkness of this age, against spiritual hosts of wickedness in the heavenly places.

EPHESIANS 6:12

Can two walk together, unless they are agreed?

AMOS 3:3

Two are better than one, Because they have a good reward for their labor. For if they fall, one will lift up his companion. But woe to him who is alone when he falls, For he has no one to help him up.

ECCLESIASTES 4:9-10

"Again I say to you that if two of you agree on earth concerning anything that they ask, it will be done for them by my Father in heaven.

MATTHEW 18:19

'For this reason a man shall leave his father and mother and be joined to his wife, and the two shall become one flesh;' so then they are no longer two, but one flesh. Therefore what God has joined together, let not man separate."

MARK 10:7-9

Chapter 2: Notes

_____

_____

_____

_____

_____

_____

_____

_____

_____

_____

THE POWER TO DEFUSE ARGUMENTS

casting down arguments and every high
thing that exalts itself against the knowledge
of God, bringing every thought into captivity
to the obedience of Christ,

2 CORINTHIANS 10:5

You're probably saying, isn't this what we've been talking about in the first two chapters: Arguing? No, it's really not. There's a difference between a disagreement and an argument. An argument is an exchange of diverging or opposite views, typically a heated or angry one. Arguments can involve negative emotions and accusations that will cause you to be defensive and cause hurt and pain.

Disagreement simply means we don't agree. It can be a positive thing; we just can't agree because we have different views.

> *"Be angry, and do not sin:" do not let the sun go down on your wrath, nor give place to the devil.*
> EPHESIANS 4:26-27

Being angry is OK. We sin when it develops into an argument involving two or more people. I can be angry and keep it to myself, but when I involve another person and words start flying around, there is disrespect, and someone's hurt in the process. It's an argument, and it's a sin. So how do we defuse this situation? There's a lot of loud noise, sometimes screaming. To diffuse this situation, it takes wisdom, maturity, insight, and of course, the Holy Spirit. When you're in a heated argument, someone filled with the Holy Ghost must stop, listen, and respond with OK when yelling occurs. I usually don't hear anything because my mind does not understand loud noises - and yelling is a loud noise. So, I just listen to the Holy Spirit, and He will speak quietly but loud enough for your Spirit to hear. There are two OKs that take place in this situation:

1. The OK to the Holy Spirit, and
2. The OK to the person opposite you either in person or on the phone.

It can be difficult at times when it's heated. We have to tell our flesh to shut up and submit to the Spirit. In some situations, you have to walk away. Because there are times when a person is yelling and can't listen to reason or even hear you say OK, sometimes, it's all about them and what they want. Their way or the highway, so take the highway and walk away.

Remember, this is not about you. It's about God being glorified first and foremost and a win-win situation. You have to protect your peace. You have to guard your heart. You have to take control over your flesh. Come on; we know it's an attack from the enemy. Put that fire out with cool refreshing water. In Proverbs 15:1, we find that *"A soft answer turns away wrath, but a harsh word stirs up anger."* We don't want to stir the pot or heat it up. Verse 2 says, *"The tongue of the wise uses knowledge rightly, but the mouth of fools pours forth foolishness."* Knowledge rightly, I like how it says rightly. We have to allow God to orchestrate knowledge so that it is used in the right manner. OK empowers us to be redirected, to reexamine the situation, to rethink, to rehearse in our hearts what the Word says, to reposition ourselves. Isn't our God great?

In defusing a situation, we have to understand who is Lord over us. The person who we are in contact with or ourselves. We say that Jesus is Lord over our lives, then it's time to let the Holy Spirit guide us.

———

I was having a conversation with one of my spiritual daughters the other day, and she said, "Pastor," I said, "OK," but then I was like OK, what? And so, she began to say that it didn't work. She was even madder than before. Well, there are two OKs. Sometimes the OK is to help you adjust your attitude and emotions, thus bringing them under subjection to the Holy Spirit. Sometimes we say OK and just be quiet because God can't move in that situation if we're operating in our flesh or emotions.

Are we just saying OK to shut the person up? No, we are saying OK to rethink or redirect or check our mindset, attitude, and emotions. We are allowing the Holy Spirit to redirect us. He, the Holy Spirit, may tell us to be quiet and not say anything, to table the conversation and come back to it later so we can get in the presence of God for instructions. The OK is not about them; it's about you and allowing yourself to receive the wisdom of God in the situation.

Even so the tongue is a little member and boasts great things. See how great a forest a little fire kindles! And the tongue is a fire, a world of iniquity. The tongue is so set among our members that it defiles the whole body, and sets on fire the course of nature; and it is set on fire by hell. For every kind of beast and bird, of reptile and creature of the sea, is tamed and has been tamed by mankind. But no man can tame the tongue. It is an unruly evil, full of deadly poison. With it we bless our God and Father, and with it we curse men, who have been made in the similitude of God. Out of the same mouth proceed blessing and cursing. My brethren, these things ought not to be so. Does a

> *spring send forth fresh water and bitter from the*
> *same opening?*
>
> JAMES 3:5-11

One of the fruits of the spirit is self-control. We have to say OK to the Holy Spirit to get that tongue under control.

One of the main components of the gifts of the Spirit is Love, and the second is self-control. Now they (the gifts) are all important, but these two are more important in these scenarios. But let's look at all of them in Galatians 5:22-23, *"But the fruit of the Spirit is love, joy, peace, longsuffering, kindness, goodness, faithfulness, gentleness, self-control. Against there is no law."* You can never have too many of these in your life as they help you as a Christian to live Christlike. So think of these when you are in a heated situation. Then, STOP! And invite the Holy Ghost in.

When I said STOP! I was reminded of the drill in school when I was a child. STOP, DROP, and ROLL. That drill kept us from getting burned. We can practice this drill in a heated situation so that neither you nor the other person will be hurt. There's a popular saying that hurting people hurt people. Stop and listen to the Holy Spirit, drop (not literally on your knees, but surrendering in your heart) what you're doing or saying, and repent of anything that has already taken place in this situation that was done in our flesh. Rollover (Ask the Holy Spirit to cause you to rethink and redirect the situation.) and come up victorious after we've received wisdom from God. That's either by being quiet or yielding to the Holy Spirit.

CHAPTER 3: NOTES

THE POWER TO DEFUSE ARGUMENTS

Scripture Readings:

Casting down arguments and every high thing that exalts itself against the knowledge of God, bringing every thought into captivity to the obedience of Christ,

2 CORINTHIANS 10:5

"Be angry, and do not sin:" do not let the sun go down on your wrath, nor give place to the devil.

EPHESIANS 4:26-27

A soft answer turns away wrath, But a harsh word stirs up anger.

PROVERBS 15:1

Even so the tongue is a little member and boasts great things. See how great a forest a little fire kindles! And the tongue is a fire, a world of iniquity. The tongue is so set among our members that it defiles the whole body, and sets on fire the course of nature; and it is set on fire by hell. For every kind of beast and bird, of reptile and creature of the sea, is tamed and has been tamed by mankind. But no man can tame the tongue. It is an unruly evil, full of deadly poison. With it we bless our God and Father, and with it we curse men, who have been made in the similitude of God. Out of the same mouth proceed blessing and cursing. My brethren, these things ought not to be so. Does a spring send forth fresh water and bitter from the same opening? But the fruit of the Spirit is love, joy, peace, longsuffering, kindness, goodness, faithfulness, gentleness, self-control. Against such there is no law. And those who are Christ's have crucified the flesh with its passions and desires.

GALATIANS 5:22-24

Chapter 3: Notes

_____

_____

_____

_____

_____

_____

_____

_____

_____

_____

THE POWER OF **OK** IN MINISTRY

He said to him the third time, "Simon, son of Jonah, do you love Me?" Peter was grieved because He said to him the third time, "Do you love Me?" And he said to Him, "Lord, You know all things; You know that I love You." Jesus said to him, "Feed My sheep.

JOHN 21:17

Well, you don't know this, but now you do. It took me a week to start writing this chapter. I really had to get in prayer. I was going through something concerning ministry, marriage, and the choice to walk by faith. It was time for a breakthrough. One thing I've never liked was a confrontation. Sometimes I used the word OK to avoid dealing with a situation. I would say OK, but never go back or deal with the situation as I figured; it'll blow over. How many times have we avoided situations saying it'll blow over, but then eventually, it comes back around? Well, I had dealt with a similar situation a few years ago and said OK to the Lord but really just kept moving, never resolving the problem, never dealing with it. I just moved on. But, in reality, I said OK and gave up, and I retreated. God did not call us to retreat or give up.

I'll let you in on a little secret.

So, this situation came back around - different person, but the same spirit. I was on repeat. How many of you have heard what you don't conquer, you will repeat? So, I retreated and had to repeat. I realized because I didn't want to deal with or didn't want to have a confrontation, that I was operating in fear. II Timothy 1:7 states, "For God has not given us the spirit of fear, but of power and of love and of a sound mind." So, I was paralyzed with fear of confrontation. Well, this time, I said, "OK. Lord, so what do I need to do?" He said, "What does confrontation have to do with what I told you to do?" I tell you that the Lord would not allow me to sleep until I confronted this thing - until I spoke up. What's so amazing about our God is He showed me in a dream what the outcome could be if I did confront the situation and what it would be if I didn't. Plus, He reminded me that fear has no control over me unless I allow it. So, that was the first OK, and then there was the second OK - the Orchestrated Knowledge. I did it right away. I spoke up and did exactly what the Lord told me to do. Well, let me tell you, it wasn't pretty. So I was under the assumption that once I did this, it would be smooth sailing. Not so! Just because we obey God doesn't mean it will always feel good and cool and smooth as chocolate ice cream.

But when I said OK to the Lord, that meant I trusted the process.

If I tell you the fiery darts that came with my obedience, this was a time of endurance, trust, and stretching.

> *And we know that all things work together for good*
> *to those who love God, to those who are the called*
> *according to His purpose. For whom He foreknew,*
> *He also predestined to be conformed to the image of*

His Son, that He might be the firstborn among
many brethren.

ROMANS 8:28-29

So even though it didn't feel good (my flesh was crying out), I had to allow the Holy Spirit to stretch and conform me in God's image. And I tell you, it gave me life. Had I not said OK and listened to the Holy Spirit, the ministry, my marriage could have taken a turn for the worse.

So, let's talk about OK in ministry. In ministry, nine times out of ten, there will always be someone who will try to tell you how to serve or run your department. But let's say you're not serving in a department but just attending church. Even on your job, this is your workplace ministry.

One of my favorite scriptures is Ephesians 6:5-8,

Bondservants (employees serving in state or church), be obedient to those who are your masters according to the flesh(Boss or Ministry leader), with fear and trembling, in sincerity of heart, as to Christ; not with eyeservice, as men-pleasers, but as bondservants of Christ, doing the will of God from the heart, with goodwill doing service, as to the Lord, and not to men, knowing that whatever good anyone does, he will receive the same from the Lord, whether he is a slave or free (unbeliever or believer).

I'm going to talk about two different scenarios, one in the workplace and one in the church. I first learned this term at church and then used it in the workplace. For example, in 2006, I worked for a cell phone company. I started as a customer service representative and transitioned to an inventory specialist. A lot of changes took place in this particular cell phone store. We had a new manager, who was younger than I was, but nevertheless, I learned to submit under her leadership and authority. Of course, I had been an inventory specialist way before she started. I had a routine, and it worked well.

Until, well, let's say we didn't quite see eye to eye. We were like oil and water. So, one day I had a huge shipment - the largest of all time. She wanted me to train someone that day to take in the shipment. I said, "I don't have a problem teaching them, but today is not a good day because I have a lot of inventory, and it's going to take me until the end of my shift to finish it. If I train him today, I won't finish on time and can't stay late because I have to pick up my daughter from work." She said, "Well, he needs to be trained!" So I remember what

I learned, and I said OK. I even said, "OK, Lord!" The Lord reminded me just to say OK and be obedient to my master as it's not about me; it's about Him being glorified. So, I did as she asked and trained him. Of course, I didn't finish, but I was also obedient in leaving at the end of my shift, leaving her to finish the inventory. I didn't argue; I didn't fuss. I just said OK. I left in peace. The young man was trained and even helped her finish the shipment. Needless to say, they had to stay over to finish. But I was obedient.

Now I'm going to say this. There's a time when your boss may be dead wrong about things or even operating in a "not-so-integral character." But, just be obedient to God and your boss; God will get the glory. This same boss had taken a new phone illegally. She asked me to give her a new phone and a battery, saying she would bring it back the next day. I said OK, but I also took a picture of the phone and the battery and signed the day she took it with a witness and had him sign. (The young man I trained). Well, she didn't bring it back in time. About one week later, when I asked about the phone, she said, "Oh, I'll bring it back in a few days." Well, guess who showed up unexpectedly? The general manager. And when he arrived, he needed to use my desk while I was in my manager's office in a meeting. And low and behold, what did he find while sitting on my desk - the copy of the phone and battery with the signatures of both my coworker and me? So I come out of the office, and he is at my desk with the paper in hand.

I'm like, OK, Lord. So, of course, he asked me what the paper was, and I had to tell him. Unfortunately, she was relieved of her duties. I was very sad for her because it didn't have to go that way. With leadership comes responsibility, accountability, integrity, and maturity. We have to surrender to God in every area of our lives. I was obedient, even when I knew it was wrong, but I had a witness to prove that I did my part. I did find out going forward that I needed to bring that to their attention if it ever happened again.

———

So, let's talk about OK in the ministry. Both of these are ministries because it's all in service and obedience to God! At my church, I learned about OK in ministry as a Service Administrator (SA). A service administrator ensures the service runs smoothly and on time, as much as possible. The SA communicates with several departments and pastors within the church service to inform them how the service is going before they enter the sanctuary. I would give each department an order of service cards with the times they were to serve in whatever capacity they were assigned. Again, there's always one who wants to tell you how to do your job - got to love them!

They are there to stretch you, to teach you how to endure. This tool of OK was genius for this position and introduced me to use this in my walk with Christ.

It's a life tool if used properly, but, as we discussed in the previous chapters, it can also be a wrecking ball. It can be condescending, disrespectful, and a tool to say I don't want to hear it. So, I can recall several instances at church during my service as an SA when some people would try and tell me how to do things. So I would say OK, thank you so much, and did what I knew I was led to do by the Holy Spirit. They left happy and empowered, and I was satisfied knowing I was obedient to the Holy Spirit. As a result, the service was a success. I started being a SA when a sister in the church had to serve at another location. So, I passed it on, and God grew that ministry within the church. I'm sure they're still using it today. It worked so well that I used it as a tool to diffuse arguments in counseling marriages and in my relationships.

CHAPTER 4: NOTES

THE POWER OF OK
IN MINISTRY

Scripture Readings:

He said to him the third time, "Simon, son of Jonah, do you love Me?" Peter was grieved because He said to him the third time, "Do you love Me?" And he said to Him, "Lord, You know all things; You know that I love You." Jesus said to him, "Feed My sheep.

JOHN 21:17

For God has not given us a spirit of fear, but of power and of love and of a sound mind.

II TIMOTHY 1:7

And we know that all things work together for good to those who love God, to those who are the called according to His purpose. For whom He foreknew, He also predestined to be conformed to the image of His Son, that He might be the firstborn among many brethren.

ROMANS 8:28-29

Bondservants, be obedient to those who are your masters according to the flesh, with fear and trembling, in sincerity of heart, as to Christ; not with eyeservice, as men-pleasers, but as bondservants of Christ, doing the will of God from the heart, with goodwill doing service, as to the Lord, and not to men, knowing that whatever good anyone does, he will receive the same from the Lord, whether he is a slave or free.

EPHESIANS 6:5-8

Chapter 4: Notes

_____

_____

_____

_____

_____

_____

_____

_____

_____

_____

THE POWER OF SAYING **OK** TO THE HOLY SPIRIT

However, when He, the Spirit of truth, has come, He will guide you into all truth; for He will not speak on His own authority, but whatever He hears He will speak; and He will tell you things to come.

JOHN 16:13

aying OK to the Holy Spirit seems simple right? Well, we can say sure it is, but when the time comes, our flesh does not want to obey. I've been using the term OK for quite some time but didn't realize I only used it in fairly easy situations. For example, I recently encountered a situation and was having a conversation with myself and God. I would always say, "I don't like confrontation."

I said this quite often and used the term OK to get out of confronting situations, or sometimes I'd do the right thing and seek God for what to do next.

In a recent situation, I knew there would be a confrontation if I said something. Most of the time, I'd pray, "Lord, whatever you would have me to say to this person, prepare their heart to receive it or reveal it to them." In this instance, the Lord spoke to me, saying, "You always say you don't like confrontation, but what does that have to do with your obedience to me?" Well, that was an eye-opener. I said, "OK, Lord, you're right." But I still did not do what he told me to do. I said, "OK," but was still reluctant because, again, I didn't like confrontation. The Holy Spirit revealed that I was walking in fear. And we know that II Timothy 1:7 says,

"For God has not given us a spirit of fear, but of power and of love and of a sound mind."

The spirit of the fear of confrontation entered in. What I had to confront was detrimental to my marriage and ministry, so I had to do it. Let me tell you that if the Lord tells you to say something, you better say it. I'm telling you, I didn't sleep for two nights. On the morning of that second night, the Lord revealed to me in a dream that if I didn't say what he told me to say, what I dreamed about couldn't come to pass. The dream was amazing.

When I woke up that morning, I knew I'd better be obedient to the Holy Spirit. So I said, "OK, Lord, I will do it." Now normally, when I'm obedient to the Holy Spirit, it is smooth sailing, everything is peaceful, and everything turns out great. The person receives it right away, and we're good to go. Hmm, that's what I thought! I was obedient to the Holy Spirit, and I said what He said to say when He said to say it. And guess what? There was no smooth sailing, and there was no peace. Now it did turn out OK, but not right away. So I learned that even when saying OK to the Holy Spirit, things may not seem OK or go as smoothly as we think. We must acknowledge that our ways are not His ways. Well like Job said, the thing that I greatly feared happened. The confrontation I was faced with it;

was in my face. I was like, "WAIT, LORD, this was not what I was expecting."

Psalms 27:14 says,

> *"Wait on the Lord; Be of good courage, And He shall strengthen your heart; Wait, I say, on the Lord!"*

The Lord explained that He had to teach me how to go through the storm. See, the enemy wanted me to retreat because of the confrontation, but God said, "Not so, I'm teaching you how to face the confrontation, not with flesh and blood because we don't wrestle against flesh and blood. This thing had to be done in the spirit." In prayer and in casting that care to the Lord. Like He says in Romans 8:28,

> *"And we know that all things work together for good to those who love God, to those who are the called according to His purpose."*

It didn't feel good, but it worked out for my good. I thank God for this lesson. I thank God that I'm able to say OK to the Holy Spirit and trust the process. With the wisdom and understanding I learned and the fear I overcame, I'm no longer afraid of confrontation, especially if it's orchestrated by the Holy Ghost. I know that God hasn't given me the spirit of fear. I have the power of the Holy Ghost, and I have the power to say "Yes." I have the authority over my circumstances. Confrontation and fear can no longer rule me.

In these chapters, I'm praying that you learn to use the power of OK to rethink, reevaluate, reposition, redirect, resubmit, and resolve. I can't tell you how the power of OK has helped me control my thinking, control my tongue, and control my response. I'm now able to respond and not react. It has helped me to control my emotions and keep my peace. The Holy Spirit is so amazing! We don't say OK to brush things under the rug; we say OK to orchestrate knowledge, to redirect us to get a better understanding of how to allow God to be Lord over our lives.

Think of an orchestra conductor; they direct the musicians when to play their instruments so that the notes are right on time and the sound is perfect. They have the wisdom and understanding of each sound and note.

———

Again, the O in OK is Orchestrate: to direct your thoughts and plans and give ear to the Holy Spirit. The K in OK is knowledge:

once you direct your thoughts, plans, and ear to the Holy Spirit, you receive the wisdom and knowledge of the Holy Spirit on what your next plan of action will be. So, the next time you want to debate, argue, or react, think of the power of just saying OK instead of responding. Take time to wait on the Holy Spirit to respond to your situation, and then come back and deal with it. Or just table it if you don't get an answer right away. Isn't it better to study to be quiet than to hurt with your words? Isn't it better to get instructions from our teacher and our guide? Even when we do, and it doesn't turn out the way we think it should, it is all in His hands, and He's working every situation out for our good. This way, we win in the end, OK?

CHAPTER 5: NOTES

HOW TO SAY OK TO THE HOLY SPIRIT

Scripture Readings:

However, when He, the Spirit of truth, has come, He will guide you into all truth; for He will not speak on His own authority, but whatever He hears He will speak; and He will tell you things to come.

JOHN 16:13

"For God has not given us a spirit of fear, but of power and of love and of a sound mind."

TIMOTHY 1:7

"Wait on the Lord; Be of good courage, And He shall strengthen your heart; Wait, I say, on the Lord!"

PSALMS 27:14

Chapter 5: Notes

AKNOWLEDGMENTS

want to dedicate this book to God who has given me a new life through his Son, Jesus Christ, and the guidance of the Holy Spirit.

To my Pastor, my husband, my friend, my partner in ministry and life, Pastor Stanley Jay. You have been my inspiration, my canvas on which I have been able to paint the vision and dreams that God has downloaded into me. You have pushed me to be all that God has called me to be. You have allowed me to stand by your side and walk this journey and path with faith. You've allowed me to fall and make mistakes but have been there to hold my hand and help me up. I thank you "honey bunches of oats." (Stanley Jay)

To my children, I want to thank you for allowing me to be your mom and your example. Even with my mistakes, you still trust the God in me to teach, guide and grow with you. I Love you all. Thank you for not giving up on me even when I wanted to give up on myself. For all my family and friends that have supported me in life, I love you and appreciate you all.

To my Worship Life Center Church family, thank you for your support and for trusting the God in me to impart wisdom into your life.

And to my amazing spiritual daughter who is with our heavenly Father, the Word says to be absent from the body is to be present with the Lord. Rachelle Evans, thank you for being my prayer partner, my best friend, and an amazing encourager. I miss your presence here on earth, but continue to hear your voice in my spirit telling me "Mom you got this, come on mom." I could not write this book without acknowledging you for what you've done in my life. I Love you, Rachelle Evans.

To my W.O.W. women: (Women of Worship,.) You have blessed me and encouraged me to write this book, as I imparted the power of OK to all of you in so many ways. As God downloaded His wisdom into me to pour into you, I felt we were all continuing to grow together.

Father thank you for an amazing download of wisdom from you.. I acknowledge all those who will read this book and pray it will bless their lives like it did mine.

ABOUT THE AUTHOR

PASTOR JOYCE JAY is the Co-Founder and Pastor of Worship Life Center Church in Mesa Arizona, where she is co-pastoring and is helping to transform lives through the word and ministering to numerous woman at Worship Life Center, she is the founder of W.O.W. Women Of Worship, and a Certified Life Coach.

Pastor Joyce has completed Biblical Studies at Faith School of Ministries in Corona California and Living Praise Christian Institute in Chatsworth California

Pastor Joyce was raised in Los Angeles, California and has been happily married to Pastor Stanley Jay for 19 years; they have 6 children and 16 grandchildren. Pastor Joyce has been in Ministry for over 20 years and has held countless women's groups and ministries and continues to minister to women across the nation.